Deception in Perilous Times

Robert F Paden and The Plowman

Published by The Plowman, 2022.

DECEPTION IN PERILOUS TIMES

First edition. September 1, 2022.

Copyright © 2022 Robert F Paden and The Plowman.

ISBN: 979-8215668368

Written by Robert F Paden and The Plowman.

I dedicate this book to America! the land of the free and the home of the brave! The biblical concepts included in the constitution have been like a beacon to guide us to what we aspire to be as a nation.

CHAPTER ONE
Deception, The Greatest Danger in Life

Jesus said, "Beware that you not be deceived!" He said that in the context of his disciples' question, "What will be the sign of your coming and the end of the age?" He was warning us that deception would become more and more a <u>major problem</u> at the end of the age. The apostle Paul, inspired by the Holy Spirit, also warned us that in the later days <u>perilous times</u> would come. It is becoming more and more evident that we are now living in perilous times. <u>T</u>he greatest peril we face is <u>deception in all its forms,</u> because <u>if you are deceived,</u> and turn away from the truth, <u>you become a party to those that are enemies of God.</u> The battle takes place in the mind, and that is where it is won or lost. The Lord wants us to be guided by the truth, but many are guided by *their <u>perception</u>* of what the truth is, and that can be very false!

GOD IS FAITHFUL IN DIFFICULT TIMES

The promises of God are certain and sure and our part is to believe and obey even when we are facing difficulties and we can't see "the end of the tunnel". Sometimes the difficulties seem impossible to surmount. Things happen that we don't expect, but that does not change God's perspective nor his plans for us.

God promised the Israelite's when they were slaves in Egypt that he would take them to a promised land flowing with milk and honey, (great abundance!) There was nothing or no one that could stop them from taking possession of that land! Hebrews 4:3 states that "The works were finished from the foundation of the earth!" The peoples of Canaan were trembling and already defeated! However, only Joshua and Caleb and those under twenty years of age finally entered in to the land. Verse six tells us that they to whom it was first preached entered not because of unbelief!

In I Corinthians 10;1-6 Paul said, "Brethren, I would not have you ignorant how our fathers were under the cloud and <u>all</u> passed through the sea. And they <u>all</u> ate of the same spiritual meat, and did drink of the same spiritual drink for they drank from that rock that followed them and that rock was Christ! But with many of them God was not well pleased: for they were overthrown in the desert."

The figures of the cloud and the sea were symbols of baptism in water and in the Holy Spirit. They saw the miracles but did not receive the promise. God did some tremendous miracles to bring his people out of slavery. Then he gave them food and drink in the desert and gave them victory over their enemies. But most of them practiced complaining instead of being thankful and marveling at the mighty hand of God!

God let them taste of hardness in the desert to prepare them for the battle to conquer the promised land. The hardness they suffered on the way had its purpose. They needed to be prepared. But they wanted to return to Egypt and eat the melons and garlic of Egypt! They forgot about the slavery and the whips of the cruel masters. Every time they complained their faith was diminished and the deceit increased. So that when they had to confront the giants in the land of Canaan (something they hadn't expected) they were afraid. They forgot about all the promises, even though the works of God were finished from the foundation of the world! They could have entered in!

<u>Joshua and Caleb were not deceived</u> because they were firm in the faith. They said, "If the Lord <u>delight in us</u>, then he will bring us into this land, and give it to us; this land that flows with milk and honey!" (Numbers 14:8) In the end, only Joshua and Caleb and those under twenty years old entered in to the land. The others all fell in the desert! For us also is that promise, "If the Lord delight in us", he will give us the victory!

Paul exhorts us in I Corinthians 10:6 "Now these things were <u>our examples </u>that we should not lust after evil things as they also lusted." Human nature hasn't changed and God doesn't change. In us also as in the Israelite's, disobedience and the lack of gratefulness will let Satan's deceit get in, even though the promises of God are yea and amen. We will receive if we do not let deception turn our heads. Let us learn all that God wants to teach us. Many times, as with the Israelite's, we are faced with the unexpected and hardness; something we did not plan for. That is the time to remember of God's faithfulness.

DECEPTION IN THE GARDEN OF EDEN

Deception has been a problem since the beginning, even in the Garden of Eden. Eve, who had never known want or hunger or any of the hard things that can touch our lives today, was deceived by the devil to believe she was missing something. "God was hiding something from them that would make their lives more meaningful. They would be as gods!" The master of deception made her dissatisfied with their present life.

Deception is like that. We are deceived to think that we are missing something that we really deserve; life will somehow be more meaningful or we will have more power or more money if we follow a certain philosophy and throw off the chains of this present authority. Then we will achieve that thing! Sometimes it's not even external authority, but what we know deep down that we should do, or shouldn't do. In deception, there is always someone or something that is "unjustly" keeping us from achieving or receiving that special thing. That is why the Scripture always exhorts us to be thankful and to give thanks in all things. God will make even the worst of circumstances turn out for good, if we trust him. Not only that, but the lessons we are supposed to be learning today are to prepare us for future overcoming!

What happened in the Garden seems impossible! They were living in paradise! They had perfect bodies, and perfect nutrition. They were king and queen, masters of their universe! Deception and the human mind is an interesting study. In Eve's case, it provoked her to rebel, and Adam followed suit. She said, "God hath said, Ye shall not eat of it (the fruit of the tree in the midst of the garden) nor shall ye touch it lest ye die."

She added the part of not touching the fruit. God did not say that they couldn't touch the fruit. As she started gazing at it, the appeal became stronger and stronger. Satan's words, "You will be as gods!" were ringing in her ears. The deception kept increasing until it overcame the warning that they shouldn't eat that particular fruit. Perhaps she even touched it and nothing happened! That would prove that God was lying to them! The deception becomes complete! And she ate it! And they ate it! And they fell!

Adam should have taken authority over the situation and said, Let's go somewhere else and enjoy a good meal that is sanctified by the word of God. But he didn't. He ate it with her. God had spoken to Adam about this, not Eve. He became not only a party to the sin, but responsible. Sin entered into the human race through Adam. The male sons of Adam pass on the sin nature, not the females. That is why the virgin Mary did not pass the sin nature to Jesus.

We shall see how deception can begin to rule over even an <u>entire nation.</u> It seems impossible what people will do under the spell of deception. Jesus <u>first</u> comment to his disciples' question about the end of the age was "Take heed that no man deceive you!" We live in an age of deception as never before. *Paul spoke of the coming of the "man of sin" "Even him whose coming is after the working of Satan with all power and signs and lying wonders, and with all deceivableness of unrighteousness in them that perish; because they received not the love of the truth, that they might be saved. And for this cause God shall send them <u>strong delusion</u> that they should believe a lie: That they all might be damned <u>who believed not the truth, but had pleasure in unrighteousness.</u>"* (2 Thessalonians. 2:9-12)

Down through the ages <u>deception</u> has been a major factor in the sin of mankind. And we can see some of the same tactics of Satan when he attempts to overthrow God's authority. Man becomes a pawn in the hands of Satan. That does not make him innocent of sin. The apostle Paul had it right when he said, "We wrestle not with flesh and blood but with spiritual wickedness in high places." (Ephesians 6:12) Satan manipulates mankind like the puppeteer with his puppets. Even the evilest people are puppets in the hands of the spiritual puppeteers (demons).

Jesus said while hanging on the cross, *"Father, forgive them! They know not what they do!"* They didn't know? Yes, they knew what they were doing, but they were deceived into believing that it was for the greater good. (They were going to preserve the nation of Israel!) Of course, by what they did, Jesus purchased our salvation, but that wasn't what they had in mind. <u>God in his mercy and sovereignty can work good out of the worst things the devil can do.</u> The human mind can rationalize even the worst evils known to man. That's why we must be careful to seek and know the truth, <u>especially as the end draws near.</u>

Jesus said, *"If you <u>dwell</u> in my Word, you will be my disciples and you shall know the TRUTH and the truth shall set you free!"* (Jn. 8:32) When we come in to the kingdom from the world, we all need to be set free! We need to gird up our loins with the truth. Deception is universal in the world. We all have been deceived to a certain extent. The world and its wisdom are mistaken! The Word of God is truth and will set us free from the lies, half lies, superstitions and fears of the world and our culture, if we abide in it. We must remember that our knowledge of good and evil was gotten through sin and is very imperfect. We need for God to tell us and show us what is right and wrong. That is why we need to dwell in His Word to be set free.

Paul said "Be ye transformed by the <u>renewing of your mind</u> that you may prove what is the good and perfect will of God!" (Romans. 12:2) The world is deceived. Many of the old sayings we knew so well were not from the Word of God. Superstitions and fears that keep people in bondage are not founded in truth. Proverbs 14:12 says, *"There is a way that seems right to man but the end thereof are the ways of death."* That is why we need to renew our mind by learning the Word of God and putting it to practice. Even minor sins and habits can lead to greater sins. Satan speaks to us through demons who "whisper in our ears". Many evil suggestions that pop into our heads are planted there by demons. And many people will suggest evil things! "Of such turn away!" (2Timothy. 3:5) And, "Walk not in the counsel of the ungodly. (Psalm 1:1)

However, in this study we will concentrate on how deception can overcome even an entire people, or "mob psychology". In an emotional moment an entire mob can be convinced to do something that they would never do when they have time to think about it. Also, an entire nation or even nations can be deceived through indoctrination and "brainwashing". We must love truth!

CHAPTER TWO
Guardians of the Word or False Teachers?

The Sadducees in the time of Jesus were modernists. They said "the Scripture doesn't really mean what it looks like it means." Does that sound like what some "progressive" churches are saying today? The party of Pharisees, on the other hand was formed to bring Israel back to the Word of God. They were fundamentalists! The Jewish people who came back from captivity didn't know the Scriptures, so the Pharisees would teach the people the Word to keep them from falling away!

But being guardians of the Word, they began to deceive themselves and add little details to the Word to make sure the people obeyed. Since they were in charge of the Word, they could use it for their own purposes and even to line their pockets. Some added houses stolen from widows to their "portfolio". They justified their actions saying that these were gifts to God and they would receive them as God's stewards! A deceiver has to deceive himself first! They were deceiving themselves. Liars believe their own lies.

THEY BELIEVED in The Coming of The Messiah, and they thought of course he would come through the party of the Pharisees. They were very proud and assumed they would be the first to be advised of his coming! When Jesus was born in Bethlehem, the wise men from the East asked king Herod where to find the new king, thinking the king would be the first to know. But of course, he didn't know the Scriptures, and had to ask the religious leaders. They knew immediately where the Messiah was to be born. <u>They knew the Scriptures by heart</u> but instead of being corrected and guided by the Word, they cleverly used it to justify their own actions.

They didn't bother to go to Bethlehem (though it is not far from Jerusalem the capital) to check it out because of course they were so sure that when he came, they would be the first to know about it. The truth is that God was giving them an opportunity to be among the first to know about the birth of the Savior, but they were already in deception! They were convinced that these strangers from the East could not have known about the coming of the Messiah before they did!

We condemn them, but do we realize that God might do some things just a little bit differently now in the end times than we have imagined? God is God and Jesus is Lord and we don't always understand so perfectly all that God has planned, but if we are diligent and study the Word, God will reveal to us what we need to know <u>when we need to know it</u>. It's a matter of humility. We do not always understand what God is doing at the moment but if we trust Him, we can be at peace and He will show us in good time.

Each denomination has its doctrines and patterns, some of which have been passed down for generations. But are they always based purely on the Word of God? And are we aware that God may move in a way that we do not expect? Jesus did not fit in to the pattern that even many of the best Hebrew scholars had for him. He was poor and humble and did not raise up an army to overthrow the cruel Roman occupation. And when he was born, God notified the poor shepherds out on the hills first! Then God revealed to Simeon and Anna that Jesus was the Messiah when Joseph and Mary took him to the temple. Meanwhile, the majority of the people were ignorant of the birth of their king!

The deception of the Pharisees and Scribes (professors) and Sadducee's and priests only increased as time went on. When Jesus began his ministry, the fulfillment of many prophecies unfolded in front of their very eyes! They didn't want to admit that they were wrong, so they majored on minors. They looked for any little thing for which they could accuse Jesus. They were jealous of him and his popularity and they were afraid they would lose their place of prestige and power.

Why was Jesus so hard on them, especially the Pharisees? Because they had the Word of God, and they were responsible, at least in part, for the spiritual welfare of their people. But their attitude was wrong and they wouldn't believe what the Word said, nor were they subject to it! They proclaimed themselves to be the "guardians of the faith!" But observe how their self-deception increased! They came to the point of thinking they could kill Jesus, contrary to the law in order to prove to the people that he was not the Messiah!

However, the evidence of who he was kept increasing and their deception kept increasing. They wanted to throw him down the cliff or stone him, and finally they turned him over to the Romans to be crucified. They thought, "If he dies, that just proves that he is not the Messiah!"

In all this, they were very careful to observe the law! (Self-deception) When Judas returned the thirty pieces of silver to the priests and Pharisees which they had given him to betray Jesus, they had no pangs of conscience about what they had done and even debated what would be the "righteous thing" to do with that money because it was "blood money". They convinced themselves that they were obeying the law perfectly! Also, when they took Jesus to Pilate to certify his death sentence, they wouldn't go into the Roman court yard because "that would defile them". (They were holy) Their deception was complete. We should examine ourselves carefully in the light of this that our motives are pure and that we truly desire to walk in the truth!

Jesus had warned them sternly. He said, *"Generation of vipers! Who will save you from the fires of hell!?"* (Mathew. 23 esp. vs33) He also warned Judas before his betrayal that it would have been better for him not to have been born than to betray his teacher. (Mt. 26:24, Mark. 14:21) And when Judas kissed him in the garden to identify him, Jesus said, "<u>Friend</u>, do you betray me with a kiss?" God is not willing that any should perish, <u>but many do</u>. Judas had also believed in Jesus, but his belief was based on an ideology of the superiority of Israel with Jesus as its king! He could not accept the apparent weakness and humility of Jesus and his disregard for riches. (John. 12:3-8 and 13:5-18) He also thought he would make some "good money" by betraying him. Jesus would probably squirm out of this anyway, just like he always did. In the garden, Jesus still called him friend! Was it to give him one last chance?

THE DECEPTION GROWS and takes control of the crowd in the courtyard of Pilate! Many of those same people had followed Jesus when he was teaching. Many had been healed or set free from demons. Many had acclaimed his entry into Jerusalem just a few days before, crying Hosanna! Blessed is he that comes in the name of the Lord! The crowd acclaimed him!

But then they were disillusioned. They had expected him to take control and assert his kingship! Their hope was misplaced of course and "Hope deferred makes the heart sick". The Pharisees took advantage of that. They were experts in crowd psychology and sent instigators into the crowd to convince them to shout, "Crucify him, crucify him!" It was a dark day of deception!

After the Resurrection, (Acts 2:37), some of those same people were amazed when they saw the miracle of the lame man healed. They could not deny his healing and realized that this man, lame from birth, was jumping for joy! Peter used that miracle as proof that God had indeed raised Jesus from the dead! They were *pricked in their heart*, remembering that they too had cried, "*Crucify him, crucify him*". They had been a part of Jesus' condemnation! They had been under deception, but as they repented, God in his mercy saved many of them! What happened to those people is not unique. Many people have acted under the power of deception down through the ages. The greatest danger in these "*Perilous Times*" in which we live is deception! Many people are parroting one thing, or many things, without thinking it through, and are not unlike those people, crying slogans that are distortions of the truth.

Humility helps us not to be deceived. It is better to say concerning our interpretation of the Word, or of current events, that there are some things we may not understand yet. God forbid that we should think we know all the Truth and yet not realize what God wants to do. If we are diligent to study the Word, God will reveal to us what we need to know when it is time. <u>Trying to make all the Scriptures agree to "our doctrine" can lead to spiritual deception.</u> All the Christian cults use the Scriptures to support their beliefs. But they always take it out of context. Ideologies are taking hold in the world today, governing people's thinking, sometimes even among those who regularly attend churches.

After Jesus had fasted for 40 days, Satan used the Scriptures to tempt him, but Jesus rightly used the Scriptures to refute those false claims and temptations. He also said *"Man shall live by every word that comes out of the mouth of God."* (Mathew. 4:4) The Scriptures interpret Scriptures and we need to compare Scripture with Scripture to better understand the balance of what God wants to teach us. Extreme doctrines are brought into focus as we compare other Scriptures. The examples in the lives of the people in the Scriptures also help us to understand what God wants to teach us. The Scriptures themselves teach us to *"prove all things, hold fast to that which is good. Abstain from all appearance of evil."* (I Thessalonians. 5:21-22)

Always when the Scriptures are used to support something false, they are <u>taken out of context</u> or key words are ignored. An important axiom is "a text out of context has no pretext". Also, arguing about the meaning of the Word usually only tends to polarize each side. It is better to hold your peace and study some more. It is good to remember that the <u>Word of God does not change just because of what men say.</u> Nor does the Word of God change to fit our ideas or doctrines. The apostle Paul said, "Let God be true and every man a liar." (Romans 3:4) No matter how many people claim a certain doctrine or how long they have believed it; that in itself does not make it true. Jesus said to the pharisees, If you believe that I Am, I Am, and if you don't believe that I Am, I Am. No matter what people think or say, it does not change the truth of God's Word.

CHAPTER THREE
The Deception of the Nazis

Adolf Hitler was a great orator. People were mesmerized by his speeches. The devil himself gave him power over the people, but evidently there was an open door in that society to believe him. He taught that the Ariel race (the tall blond Germans) was superior and that they could dominate the world! But they had to eliminate the weak and sickly and exterminate the Jews, because the "Jews controlled the money and kept the common people poor". The German economy was in bad shape when Hitler began to get a foothold in power, which perhaps influenced people to want a change. The doctrine of the superior race began to be accepted throughout the German society, especially among the young people. Even though Hitler himself had dark hair and was short (not at all like the Ariel race)!

Not only the men, but the women also were deceived and took part in the terrible plan to dominate the world. The deception was taking root in many of the people of the German society. They were told that they must work to "purify" their race.

Genealogies were traced to mate husband and wife of those who came from several generations of the "Ariel" race. Then they were rewarded with certain subsidies if they had four or more children. Their goal was to have eight children and raise soldiers for the German army. To birth and raise children for the Third Reich (Third Empire) was to be one of the great contributions the women could make. Beautiful tall blond women were recruited to birth children for the Third Reich. The State would raise them and prepare them.

But there were some who resisted......

SOFIA MAGDALENA SCHOLL (1921-1943) with her brother Hans worked with the Resistance in Germany. They called the group, "The White Rose". They were tried, condemned and beheaded in 1943 for spreading anti-Nazi propaganda. She said this before she died: *"How can we expect righteousness to prevail when there is hardly anyone willing to give himself up individually to a righteous cause.—Such a fine sunny day and I have to go, but <u>what (will) my death matter, if through us thousands of people are stirred to action?</u>*

Another excellency word from Sofia:

"The real damage is done by those millions who want to survive, the honest men who just want to live in peace, those who don't want their little lives disturbed by anything bigger than themselves, those with no sides and no causes, those who won't take the measure of their own strength for fear of agonizing their own weakness, those who don't like to make waves or enemies, those for whom **freedom, honor, truth** *and* **principles** *are <u>only literature</u>, those who live small, die small. It's the reductionist approach to life. If you keep it small, you keep it under control. If you don't make any noise, the bogey man won't find you, but it's all an illusion because they die too, those people who roll up their spirits into tiny little balls so as to be safe. Safe? From what? Life is always on the edge of death. Narrow streets lead to the same place as wide avenues and a little candle burns itself just like a flaming torch does. I choose my own way to burn."*

I read an eyewitness account of Hitler's speeches. As was customary, he would speak from a high balcony overlooking the plaza. The large crowd of people would be mesmerized by his speeches and stand in awe when he spoke. As the speech gained momentum, his voice would get higher and higher until it was like the scream of a woman. The people would be totally captivated, gazing up to the balcony. He had a demonic power over them.

The deception continued and grew. This author knew a Christian brother who came from Germany after the war. He was a couple years older than I, about nine years old in 1941, old enough to understand many things but too young to serve in the army. He told me how the deception took hold of many in Germany. He said, "Christians who before the war would not even think of going to a movie because it was sin, when they were recruited and trained in the army, (*and under that terrible deception)* thought nothing of going into a village under orders and killing everyone there!" (His words, the emphasis mine) Also, the penalty for not obeying orders was death. Many thousands were summarily shot for disobedience.

Hitler's doctrine was to eliminate the sickly or mentally retarded. Young women and girls were also recruited to work for the Reich in that process. "They were out to dominate the world!" The work in the hospitals was important. Nurses cooperated in giving overdoses to those to be eliminated. Others were left to starve. One huge hospital that normally had 15,000 patients ended up with only 1500. The women nurses worked diligently to accomplish this. During the war, women were recruited to work in the concentration camps and in the elimination of Jews and other "undesirables". Women escorted prisoners to the gas chambers and helped them to undress. All for the Reich!

HOW DID THAT HAPPEN? Partly because too many good people took the "reductionist approach to life". Those ordinary working people that try to "keep it small, so we can handle it". Then it was too late! The church had not fulfilled its purpose to be the prophetic voice in Germany even though many Germans considered themselves to be Christians. The apostle Paul taught that "*All who will live godly in Christ Jesus shall suffer persecution.*" (2 Timothy 3:12) Nobody likes persecution. And sometimes the stakes are very high. As Hitler began to have more power, to cross him and his purposes could mean death. He "eliminated" many of those who would cross him.

But <u>had there been</u> more Sofia Scholls perhaps things would have been different. What she said on the day of her death in effect was, "There are things worth dying for!"

WINSTON CHURCHILL was called to serve in the English government late in the game after Chamberlain, England's former prime minister, had allowed Hitler to take over much of Western Europe. Churchill fortified his people in the face of an eminent takeover by German forces. He said; *"We shall neva (never) give in nor give up! We shall go to the end! We shall fight in France; we shall fight in the seas and in the oceans. We shall fight with more and more confidence and strength in the air. We shall defend our island at any price. We shall fight on the beaches and in the seaports, in the fields and in the streets. We shall fight in the mountains and we shall neva, neva, neva give up!"* His courage and leadership galvanized the British people to hold back the German army and air force until help came from the US and other allied forces even though the Germans had far superior forces at that time.

In Germany, women were put in charge of the women prisoners of war. Many that were from humble backgrounds were puffed up with pride when they were given total authority over these prisoners even to the point of life and death. Corrie Ten Boom in her book about her time as prisoner in the prison camp told about the cruelty of the women guards. Her sister and many others died because of the cruel practices and lack of medical attention. Her father died soon after he was taken captive. Her brother was never heard from again after his capture. The Jewish prisoners were sent directly to the death camps. She said the guards claimed to be Christians! The deception had reached its maximum. It seemed the entire nation was under deception!

THE PLAN TO ANNIHILATE THE JEWISH PEOPLE and with them all the "undesirables" was no secret in the German society. The officer in charge of Auschwitz, the largest and most efficient killing camp, lived with his wife and children in a luxury home within earshot of the screams of the people being tortured inside the camp. They regularly used some of the prisoners as servants in their household. They taught their children that the Jews were not really human and even that "they don't feel pain like we do!"

The sickly and especially the mentally ill must be eliminated. Also, doctors were experimenting with people as if they were guinea pigs. The glorious new world they were creating justified the cruelty and the elimination of people by the millions. They had a very efficient machine to eliminate people by now.

Not all were deceived, however. Besides those that bravely formed a "resistance", to work towards the overthrow of this terrible regime that held the nation in an iron grip, some of the top German generals began to see that it was not right and even plotted to assassinate Hitler. They were not successful and were promptly "eliminated". Other things happened. A Dutchman who worked as the driver of a Rolls Royce limousine was transporting four top generals one night and knowingly took a road at high speed that terminated at the edge of a cliff, sending the car and all its occupants to their death in the river far below. He paid the ultimate sacrifice to resist the evil regime. General Rommel, one of the most brilliant German generals committed suicide. His defeat in Africa weighed upon him, but perhaps he also saw the error that they were in.

Hitler himself became more and more erratic. It is said that during the last days of the war, he would be ranting to his generals and would start to foam at the mouth and even fall down and start chewing the corner of the rug. Satanic powers had given Hitler power over the people, but now he was being destroyed by those same powers. The "deceiver" was also deceived. But by then his power structure that he had built was so complete that no one dared to raise a hand against him. Perhaps fear had come in and added to the power of deception.

Even after all hope of winning the war was gone and it was obvious that the end was near. Hitler's propaganda machine still held many under the deception that they would rise up and defeat the allies on every side.

The total destruction and needless loss of lives could have been avoided by an earlier surrender but <u>Hitler's sin had become a national sin.</u> The destruction of Germany was complete. Afterwards the survivors had to literally rebuild the nation from ashes. The result of deception is sin and the wages of sin is death.

CHAPTER FOUR
The Deception of Marxism

Carl Marx saw the disparity between the rich and the poor and envisioned a society in which everyone would be equal. His parents were Jewish Christians and when he began his studies at a university, he was writing Christian philosophy. But when he fell into deception, he wrote, "See this sword? I got it from the Prince of Darkness!" From then on, he began to write a new doctrine which was <u>man's salvation of man,</u> a utopia built by man, leaving God out. DECEPTION!

He taught that capitalism is like a disease and every one that is infected with it will only pass it on to their children. Because of this, in this new society in which everyone is equal and happy to share equally with everyone else, the "diseased" ones <u>have to be eliminated.</u> "THE END JUSTIFIES THE MEANS." (Like the Nazi dogma.) Lenin, who took over the movement later in Russia, taught that the Christian doctrine was "the opium of the poor people". Many young people bought into this doctrine. Young people, seeing the problems in society, tend to want to change things for the better, but lack in experience and maturity and lack of knowledge of history, but most of all, knowledge of the Word of God, which shows that the sins of mankind are the cause of the disparity and all the evils in society. When the evils of sin go unchecked by the Word of God, the justice system fails and the evil increases, many times to great extremes. Marxism seemed to be a solution.

But Marxism is not only atheistic, it is Antichrist. Carl Marx, raised in Christianity, felt that he had to eradicate Christianity and the Christ of Christianity because it presented an opposing solution to man's problems. The similarities between Marxism and the Nazi doctrine are no accident (totalitarianism, elimination of all who disagree) because

Satan was behind both doctrines. <u>He wants to destroy God's rule and establish his own.</u> The Bible of course teaches that man is sinful and selfish and therefore a common ownership of everything will never work. For that reason, the Communist doctrine demands that God and the Bible be eliminated as well.

Unregenerate man will never willingly share equally with everyone else nor will he work hard to compensate for those who work less. Perhaps Marx copied the example of Jerusalem at the birth of the Christian church where the people had "all things in common". However, God was doing a special thing at that time and moved those that had extra houses or properties to sell them and give the money to the apostles. <u>This supplied the need of the foreigners</u> who had come to Jerusalem to worship God and then stayed after the first great infilling of the Holy Spirit on Pentecost day. The apostles were re-interpreting the Scriptures of the Old Testament (coming to a more complete understanding) in the light of the redemption of Christ.

This was the birthing of the new church and representatives from many nations were there and preparing to take it back to their homes. God used that situation to prepare them to spread the gospel over a wide area in just a few years. The willing sharing of goods among Christians as an act of love and under the urging of the Holy Spirit is not to be compared with forcefully taking money away from the rich and giving it to the poor as the Communists do. Communism requires a very strong and merciless police and army to enforce their doctrine. In Jerusalem however, God was dealing with his newly redeemed people to share out of love in that special occasion.

The Nazis under Hitler's deception started a bloody revolution and bloody wars that perhaps in its totality killed 75 million people. Marxism or Communism has killed twice that many and is still at it! Mao Se Tun, who helped start the Communist party in China and led the revolution that took over China was a man without mercy. His wife was just as bad. When the revolution was just getting started, he and his wife were hiding from the nationalists under a bridge and their new-born baby began to cry. To avoid discovery, he told his wife to drown the baby, which she did. The end justifies the means! With the promise of a utopia, he beguiled the people.

In the villages, the Communists taught the neighbors to hate one another. They taught that the land owners were the cause of their poverty and must be killed. Hate and division was used to take total control over all the society. Brutality without mercy was used as part of the deception which spread all through China.

IDEOLOGY: *A SYSTEM THAT DERIVES IDEAS EXCLUSIVELY FROM* SENSATION (not from reason) is the type of ideology we present. Once a sector of people buy into an extreme ideology it increases in force and becomes more emotional than reasonable. Crowd psychology takes hold. Everybody is saying the same thing! And then when violence becomes part of their endeavors, the violence itself spurs them on. Deception can engulf a person's entire being. Destroying property leads to killing and killing leads to bloodthirstiness. Man as a creation of God has tremendous capacity for good, but turned away from God he has and insatiable capacity for evil. The demons take over.

Karl Marx stirred people up using the injustices in the society and promising a utopia where everyone would share equally. He taught the followers of his doctrine that the "proletariat" (the working class) would overthrow their rich oppressors and bring in the "new society". Lenin added the doctrine of destroying their oppressors with "the end justifies the means. This takes us back to the origin of deception in the Garden of Eden. Someone or something is keeping me from realizing all that should be mine. The motivating force of the Communist philosophy is always hate, envy and covetousness and not love. Marx and those that came after him taught that religion and God have to be eliminated.

Many of the rural people in Russia were not in accord with the takeover of communism. To subjugate them, their leader Lenin, and later

Stalin, took away their wheat, even their seed wheat and let them starve. Millions were starved to death. They had no seed wheat to plant a new crop. Communism's brutal hand extended to all of Eastern Europe and began to take over the Asian countries. The guerrillas would enter a village and demand immediate and total obedience to them and their doctrine. If there was resistance, they would bind the leaders of the village on the ground and run over them with tanks and trucks, thus instilling total fear and complete obedience in all the inhabitants.

<u>Indoctrination</u> was also a big part in establishing Communism. Cadres (young teachers) worked tirelessly repeating the dogmas of Communism to workers during their rest periods. Indoctrination by continual repetition begins to make an indelible impression on the mind. After a multitude of repetitions, it does not have to be true or even make sense to become a guiding principle in the minds of those who are indoctrinated. Also, the Communist strategy is always to divide the people in order to conquer them. The guerrillas were convinced they were building a new society and therefore torturing and killing the people was not only acceptable, it was necessary and desirable. The end justifies the means. DECEPTION

The Communist Party, according to their dogma is supposed to control the people until the "new generation" has learned the lessons well and the common people will take over. When Communism is complete, according to the doctrine, all the people will automatically govern themselves, each one will work to the best of his ability and receive from the common treasury according to his needs. However, the "utopia" will never come. It will never work because of man's selfish nature. The Communist Party has never and will never give up its authority and total power over the people. It always becomes a permanent totalitarian government. Man is sinful and without God, his sin and lust for power will only increase.

When Lenin died, Joseph Stalin took over the Soviet Union. He understood Lenin's philosophy perfectly and to illustrate it to his generals (it is said), he took a live chicken and picked off all her feathers one by one. Then put the poor chicken on the floor and walked ahead of the chicken, dropping corn kernels on the floor. The chicken followed him to get the corn. Stalin told his generals, "That is the way you subjugate the people!" Whether that really happened or not, in essence it is the way Communism takes over. His government was perhaps even more cruel than Leninism and his atrocities surpassed what Hitler did.

All who disagreed with him were sent to the "Gulag" (Communist work camps) It is calculated that he sent some 22 million people to the "Gulag". Millions died from starvation, sickness and overwork. He sent his armies into sure death many times. To clear a mine field, they would order soldiers to walk abreast over it, killing who it would while clearing the way for those that followed (some were recruits from the "Gulag"). It is said, Stalin lost perhaps 27 million in the war against Hitler, but it bothered him not the least. When he lost a regiment, he just inducted another and sent them into battle to be killed. It seems impossible but many people will blindly follow the very leaders who have made them to suffer but also gives them crumbs. As in Nazi Germany, death was the penalty for disobedience. Their promise of a utopia never comes.

Example: A bully beats up this little kid every day when he comes to school and takes away his lunch. Then one day the bully says to the little kid, I like you so I'm going to beat you up less every day and give you part of your lunch! The little kid is so grateful that he follows the big bully everywhere. They ask him why he follows the bully and he replies, "Because he says he likes me!" That is a made-up story but it is a reality played out over and over again.

Communism as an economic system has utterly failed. The people invariably end up living in substandard conditions. Production of all kinds is slowed down or halted altogether. Innovation (new inventions) becomes non-existent. People are taught to spy on one another. Neighborly trust disappears. Under Communism, many people die of starvation and many die for lack of medical attention. The great Soviet

Union disintegrated from within. From every Communist country people escape because of the oppression and poverty.

Communism is always destined to morph into something else because true Communism will never work. Man is selfish and each will want to have more and do less. The Communist countries always become dictatorships that subjugate the people with and iron hand. The utopia they promise never comes. They teach that there is no God and the people lose hope. In Cuba, in Venezuela, in Vietnam, in North Korea and China the people have suffered greatly. Some of the people barely live while the money is used to build up the military power and the "Elite" live in luxury. Many people become desperate to escape from those countries and risk their lives in order to escape from the tyranny of Communism. Communist countries never have a problem of immigration. In China, the "great leap forward" of Mao was a total failure.

When the great Soviet Union disintegrated, the spirit of communism did not die, it merely changed strategy. Russia, Cuba and Venezuela became outright dictatorships. In China, we now see a smiling face and they permit elections and capitalism. But there is only one party and the election is a farse. They seem to advance in technology, but much of it is stolen from other countries. The Communist Party has total power and the outside world does not see the atrocities they commit against their own people to keep them subjugated. Their strategy now is to use deception and subterfuge where possible instead of warfare in order to take over the world. American money is used to strengthen and build their power. This is facilitated by those who value money more than principles, using China's cheap labor to bolster their profits!

Many world leaders thought that opening up China to free world trade and including them in the United Nations would automatically make them change to be a democratic and free country. But they didn't understand that Communism is a spirit that doesn't die. For a time, part of the economy was opened up to free trade and with cheap labor and cheaply made production, China captivated much of the world's economic riches. Money began to flow into China, especially US money, both from buying their cheap products and from American companies' investments, lured by the cheap labor of China. But they are still Communists, with designs to take over the world. Many in the West are deceived, thinking that the socialistic system is better, but if Communism would take over the world as the Chinese Communist Party plans to do, the result would be a loss of freedom for everyone.

We need to understand that there is a difference between <u>Socialism</u> and <u>Communism</u>. Even though they are like sisters and both are based on wrong presumptions. <u>Socialism</u> is a supposedly comprised of a <u>benevolent government</u> taking care of the less fortunate in the society. We will examine that in the next chapter. Communism proports to mature into a perfect society <u>without government</u> where everyone is equal.

<u>Communism</u> will never be what their propaganda teaches, that it will "mature" into a perfect society where everyone is equal and there will be no government because everybody is sharing equally with one another and there would be no need for a governance. There will be no "sin" because it will be a "value free" society, (everyone does whatever they want). This would be total chaos, because man is sinful, but worse, in this "process" of becoming a perfect society, their doctrine says that all who have different ideas have to be eliminated. They are told that it's necessary to get rid of the evil of capitalism and Christianity which is restrictive. So, killing off people that believe in Christian principles is justified. The end justifies the means!

With cheap labor and even using slave labor in their interior, the Chinese Communist Party has captivated much of the world's economy. Many free world companies lured by riches and with few scruples have grossly enriched their top echelon people by "outsourcing" their work to the cheap labor in China. Now in the entire world there are more products sold "made in China" than the locally made products. This has brought an enormous amount of money into the hands of the Communist Party and they will use it for their ungodly purposes. They have gained control over petroleum production in some small nations. They use financial power to make the other countries mere satellites. Technology is stolen from the western world.

In China's big urban centers where it seems everything is going well, huge amounts of money are being funneled in to hands of the CCP, while the people's lives are very controlled. In their strategy to take over the world by deception, they have dozens of different propaganda and subterfuge methods to captivate the minds and hearts of people all over the world. Many young people today believe that Communism is good. They have been kept ignorant of the many atrocities committed by the Communist Party in times past and in the present time. Meanwhile in China many of the "undesirables" are held in large concentration camps and used for slave labor. The CCP makes huge profits through the sale of human organs.

They continue the design to take over the world with Communism using a much more subtle "revolution" than before. The Communist doctrine is being introduced under different names in many countries to hide its identity, but it is the same spirit of Antichrist working to deceive the people. They target the schools, the labor unions and courts of "justice". They are using internet, Hollywood, TV, children's games and sports. Psychology has also been infiltrated with the communist doctrine. <u>Dividing the people</u> and <u>changing the meaning of key words</u> are also important strategies of the Communist spirit. DECEPTION! After all that can be said about China, if there are still doubts about the intentions of the Communist Party, one should ask the people of Hong Kong, that was a free city and is now suffering under the yoke of Communism.

CHAPTER FIVE
Capitalism-Socialism-Feudalism

Socialism also pretends to distribute wealth and do away with the disparity between the rich and the poor. It is considered by many to be a compromise between communism and capitalism and a good solution for the disparity between the rich and the poor especially if those that govern are elected democratically. Socialists teach that capitalism is the cause of the inequality and poverty in the world. They define capitalism by the big corporations that gain much control over the economy. The truth is that when the corporations are hooked up with the government, it becomes more feudalism than capitalism. It becomes an aberration of Capitalism. This certainly needs to be addressed on the one hand, but Socialism has continually failed to produce a prosperous nation. "Democratic" Socialism will always have capitalism which it needs in order to maintain production in the nation, because government run production always deteriorates. Government workers have no incentive to be productive. The more the balance tends towards socialism, the more that nation suffers economically. The remedy the Socialists have for the failures of socialism however, is usually more socialism, which is a deception. Our experience in Argentina is that as the government inhibits private enterprise more and more through regulations and taxes, capitalism sprouts out "underground". Innovating people, forced out of lawful business by regulations and taxes, start a clandestine business, or begin to do two thirds of their business unreported. So, at the moment, Argentina has a national economy which is probably more than half "underground". But that's what keeps the nation on its feet!

Capitalism in its simplest form is merely <u>rules of economics</u>. It is the right of any person to own private property and to use that property for whatever purpose he likes as long as he does not infringe on the rights of others. The philosophy behind capitalism is that if a person is free to produce and reap the benefits of his production, but forced to compete with others who are free, the economic result will be more innovation and more prosperity for everyone. This may sound dangerous, but has proven to be true wherever freedom of enterprise has been allowed.

Two examples show that competition is healthy and productive. What would sports be without competition? If the result of every game was that they would both be winners, neither team would do their best. In the same way, competition in business works for the good of everyone. Also, in school, if every student received the same grade, no matter how much they learned, very soon, no one would really try to learn. In the same way, when the socialistic government provides a good income for everyone, very soon, no one will work hard to produce. Government employees also have very little incentive to do better.

Capitalism, the same as any human endeavor, needs checks and balances, just as the government does. The right and the possibility for anyone to start a business on his own, no matter who he is or how young, is the crown jewel of the virtues of capitalism. When that is lost or greatly inhibited, capitalism begins to deteriorate. It takes money to make money, so bank money at reasonable rates give a startup operation a chance. Those that have money have the advantage of a more complete operation, but a person doing his own work will do more and do it better than any employee. So, the incentive and hard work of a small endeavor helps balance his lack of money.

The huge corporations, however, <u>begin to trample on the rights of others</u>. They often skirt the tax laws and other rules that limit small businesses and gain and unfair power at the marketplace. <u>That is the very thing capitalism was designed to avoid!</u> When the big corporations get a foothold into big government, that is much more like the old feudalistic system of the dark ages than capitalism.

The founding fathers of the USA had left Europe with its monarchies, feudal systems and religious darkness which did not give equal opportunity to everyone. The peasants and serfs did all the work.

The peasants were a little better off than the serfs who were the property of their lords. Neither of those lower classes had a voice in the government and were often considered to be no more than a natural resource. Vassals were the under-lords, each in charge of a certain area. While reaping benefits from the production of that area, they protected the king's rights and enforced his authority. That was called a *Feudal* system. Although this system varied from one country to another and was ever changing as time went on, one thing remained pretty constant, the lower classes could not, except in very rare circumstances better their lot. Today we can observe how big corporations which have special advantages from the government are in fact a repetition of the old feudal system. As controls and high taxes tend to eliminate small businesses, big business takes over with special privileges they procure from interested politicians, using special lobbies as well.

When the pilgrims landed on the shores of this new country, many were strong Christians and were very conscious of the tremendous opportunity before them, given by God to lay down some righteous and godly foundations on which this new nation could be built. They were determined to live sacred lives according to biblical commands, and in so doing to build a "city upon a hill" that would be a beacon to the rest of the world. The Mayflower Compact in part reads thus:

> "For the glory of God and the advancement of the Christian faith——to plant the first colony in the northern parts of Virginia——combine ourselves together into a civil body politic, for our better ordering and preservation and furtherance of the ends aforesaid——-constitute and frame such just and equal laws, ordinances, acts, constitutions, and offices, as shall be thought most meet and convenient for the <u>general good</u> of the colony, unto which we promise all due submission and obedience."

The Puritans, and several generations (150 years) of noble-minded people took part in the forging and founding the USA. As we see, different types of social and civil systems were tried. The very Mayflower Compact was socialistic but when they found that the system didn't work, they changed it. They were fully aware of the fallen condition of man. After studying other governments and experimenting, they came up with a form of government and a form of economy that was new and different, and it has <u>surpassed all other experiments in the whole world.</u> It's a system based on the belief that common people have the capacity to form and run their own business and govern themselves, and that a free enterprise economy will work the best. This is based on the knowledge and biblical understanding that man is created in the image of God and therefore has a tremendous capacity to build a prosperous and righteous society, but also has a sin nature, so therefore <u>needs checks and balances</u> so that <u>no one or no group</u> should gain unfair advantage over the others.

This government is of the people by the people and for the people. **Government therefore, <u>does not have a purpose of its own</u>**. Its only purpose should be to serve the best interests of the people while containing the inherent evil of mankind. One of the under-girding principles of this new government was that <u>the government should only do what the people cannot do or cannot so well do for themselves.</u> Therefore, the government should not be any bigger or more powerful than necessary, and should have checks and balances, so that each part of the government is checked by the other parts.

Abraham Lincoln was very aware of this when in his Gettysburg address, he said, "Four score and seven years ago our fathers brought forth on this continent a new nation conceived in liberty and dedicated to the proposition that <u>all men are created equal!</u>"

The preamble to the Constitution reads, "*We believe that these truths are self-evident, that all men are created equal and endowed by their Creator with certain inalienable rights. That among these are <u>life, liberty and the pursuit of happiness.</u>*" Pursuit of happiness does not say that everyone will have the same, but that they have the right to <u>equal opportunity</u>. They were not blind to think that this proposition would be that easy to put into practice nor that evil men and even the sinful nature of all of us would in many different ways make very difficult the fulfillment of these premises. RATHER THAN A STATEMENT OF WHAT WE ARE, IT WAS LIKE A SHINING STAR, GUIDING US TO WHAT WE WANT TO BE AS A NATION! But they were fully aware and reiterated often that faith and obedience to God were not just important, GOD'S APPROVAL WAS ABSOLUTELY ESSENTIAL TO THE SUCCESS OF THIS ENDEAVOR.

Lincoln continued, "Now we are engaged in a great civil war, testing whether this nation, or any nation so conceived and so dedicated can long endure." The war was about slavery and the individual state's right to decide to have slavery. Slavery is as old as history and is a question that has taken much time to resolve. And though the war was won on the side to abolish slavery, *de facto* slavery continued for some time after the civil war in some areas of the South. Besides, discrimination is ever present (a human problem in this fallen world). However, the Constitution purports to help resolve these problems <u>with righteous laws</u>. The principles of God are intertwined in the Constitution. Many of our founding forefathers were God fearing men. They understood that in the gospel the love of God and love for our fellow man overcome discrimination, but that there are no short cuts to solve human problems. Today, "as we write" there exists many forms of slavery all over the world. Young girls and women are targeted and boys as well. It is underground and in its most terrible form. Righteous laws and law enforcement can go a long way to abate this evil, but only the fear of God among the people will eliminate it.

The Free Enterprise system of economics is also grounded on the principle that man is responsible and capable of taking care of himself and if he has <u>freedom</u> and <u>competition</u>, it will contribute to the general good. The failures in this system occur when someone or some entity has and unfair advantage over the other. And that is precisely why checks and balances were included in the governing system.

The following are some of checks and balances. Those who govern are <u>elected</u> in free and honest elections by the people to represent what the people need and aspire to. The powers of the government are <u>divided</u>; legislative, administrative and judiciary. The Federal government is <u>limited</u> by the state's governments. The representatives serve only <u>one term</u> at a time. Then they have to be re-elected. Citizens and news journals have a right to <u>voice their opinion</u>. That brings to light the problems that occur and need to be solved. The right to <u>bear arms</u> makes it harder for a dictator to take total control and harder for a thief to break into someone's house or rob a taxi. <u>True information</u> available for all to see and hear is of utmost importance in order to maintain a free society.

These principles of government and of economy have produced a more prosperous and freer nation than any other system in the world. Why would anyone want to change it then? **Only if they are deceived!** This government and economy were founded on biblical principles and WILL FUNCTION RIGHTLY WHEN GOVERNED BY GOD FEARING PEOPLE. They believed that this would come about only if every person had the liberty to believe in God, because <u>only love and faith freely given are truly love and faith</u>. Therefore, the Constitution prohibited the government to <u>interfere</u> in religion. The nation's righteousness and prosperity are intrinsically connected to the fear of God and obedience to the principles of the Word of God. Man in his carnal state thirsts for power and money and a truly representative government and free enterprise do not give him that advantage over his fellows that he wants, but rather limits them.

The free enterprise system is imperfect as any human system would be. As the nation drifts away from God these imperfections begin to grow. Also, as the world changes through technology and worldwide communication and transportation, many small businesses and farmers can be seriously jeopardized through no fault of their own. The markets shift and change and some machines or services are suddenly rendered obsolete. A person can have a thriving business or a productive farm and suddenly the value of his product or service is cut in half or less, or he can't sell it period! Another anomaly in our free enterprise system would be that some of the government contracts need large corporations, like the military defense budget or the manufacturing of airplanes for the airlines. Then these corporations tend to grow and grow, in some cases wiping out small businesses, or becoming a singular source of the economy in an entire region. But meanwhile with free enterprise, technology and diversity also create new jobs and businesses. Large corporations also find it better to "farm out" work to small contracting companies.

Some people are left poor because of sickness, widows left with children to raise, accidents and natural disasters, unfair business deals, and perhaps many other reasons cause some people to be left out. The Lord commanded us to help the poor among us and even promised abundant blessing on those who generously help the poor. But as people drift away from the Lord, they forget the poor and want the government to do it all. <u>So, these problems exist and need to be dealt with in some way</u>. But just because problems occur and need fixing does not mean that the system is bad. You do not throw the baby out with the bath water!

One glaring problem is political. When someone is running for office and needs money for his campaign, it is very tempting to go to big business for help. This incurs an obligation which many times starts an ungodly partnership. The politician sends some big juicy, many times grossly overpaid contracts to the "partner" and the "partner" supports him financially to stay in office. Though this is called capitalism, <u>it loses the virtue of capitalism</u>. The big corporation is no longer in competition with small business. With the government behind them, they run small businesses out of town!

The situation is not so simple. The disparity gives rise to the need for government intervention. So those who favor a socialistic government can say, see?! Capitalism fails! We need for the government to <u>control the economy</u>! But the free enterprise system has built a prosperous nation that has benefited everyone. Problems need to be addressed, but that does not mean that the system is bad. For example, if the police let a criminal escape, that does not mean we need to do away with police, and if a judge makes a bad decision, that does not mean we need to do away with the judicial system. In like manner, we need to conserve the free enterprise system while making the adjustments we need to help those left by the wayside. We will examine socialism and how a purely socialistic government tends to go from bad to worse.

Large corporations are necessary in today's world, but they need to be limited in some way and <u>forced to compete</u>. True competition will always result in benefits for the society as a whole. Some businesses and farmers and persons at some time may need help but this help should not be permanent whether it's help for a family or help for a business, it should not be eternal. What would sports be without competition? Nothing! How would students learn if everyone automatically received the same grade no matter how hard they worked and studied? Learning would go from bad to worse! It isn't money or grades in school that everyone should receive equally, it's opportunity!

The socialistic doctrine is based on <u>three false premises</u> which many people have come to accept. 1) The first false premise is that the economy of a nation is <u>like a pie</u>, static in size and value, and if one has a larger piece, it's because he has taken away from those that have smaller pieces. By this doctrine, all rich people have gotten their riches by robbing from others, so they are responsible for poverty. <u>The truth</u> of the matter however, is that GOD GAVE US THIS EARTH IN THE RAW with all its natural resources and also gave us the capacity to build, to invent, to plant and harvest. Riches and comforts as we know them are made by the hands and brains of men and multiply as man <u>plans and works</u>. If a man has a house, it's because someone built that house. If he has food to eat, it's because someone planted, harvested, prepared etc. There are only a few things you can eat in the raw, such as an apple or an orange, but even then, someone had to plant and cultivate the tree. God has ordained that the "curse" of Adam become a blessing if we abide by it. If we are willing to work and plan and save, we too will have our share of "riches".

Of course, not everyone is an entrepreneur or capable of starting a manufacturing company. Many are happy to work for someone else and let others do the worrying and planning. Meanwhile that someone else is providing work and a living for people. In a free enterprise system, there is also competition for good workers. The diligent and faithful workers tend to get better jobs and better pay. But that is not bad, everyone is encouraged to do their best and everyone benefits!

2) The second false premise is that <u>government control of the goods will be more righteous</u> than a competitive system. They forget that those that govern come from among the "unrighteous" private sector and are not suddenly more righteous because they have been elected. The fact is that the private sector is limited by competition, but the ones elected to govern now have no competition. They become the *elite*. With power and money, they become lords. When they are charged with money to "distribute", the temptation is to take part of this money for themselves, which they often do. So, they become not only the elite, but also the very rich. They work very hard to get re-elected. Often most of their time and effort is spent in getting re-elected instead of righteous governance. This must be guarded against.

3) The third false premise is that the government has its own money and should share it with the people. So therefore, it doesn't hurt the government to hand out money, they have lots of it! The truth is that the government <u>only has money that it has taken from the people </u>either in taxes or in natural resources. The nation and its natural resources <u>belong to the people.</u> So that any money a person receives from the government is being taken from the common treasury. Of course, it is not wrong for the government to give to a person who has a legitimate need. "We the people" have a common treasury for those purposes. That is in fact what

always should be the consideration whenever anyone uses government money. It's the people's money!

Socialism <u>portends</u> to equalize the incomes of everyone by government control, but historically, as socialism increases, the gap between the rich and the poor only increase. The middle class begins to disappear, as a result of being overtaxed and over controlled. The rich are allowed to get richer because the politicians need them. And since distribution of the riches is now legitimate, the politicians use some of the taxpayer's money to encourage the poor people to vote for them. Before each election they go around and promise the poor people that they will "take care of them" while blaming the rich and the "capitalists" for their poverty. People believe them and gladly take from the public treasury and it becomes a system of mass thievery and lies.

When socialism as an ideology grows, the poor section also grows. The remedy for this is more socialism. They overtax those who produce in order to "give more to the poor", and overtaxing and controls lower production capacity and put some of the producers out of business. Production grinds to a halt, unemployment grows, the national money is worth less and less because less goods and services are produced. So, the vicious circle is complete. <u>Poverty and socialism grow together</u>. The socialistic politicians <u>need</u> a big section of poor people to keep them in office. The people must be kept in ignorance because thoughtful people will see through the falseness of socialism, so the schools <u>must not teach</u> the children how to think, nor teach them history so they can judge for themselves which system is best. Instead, they use class time to indoctrinate the young people.

The graduating students that are indoctrinated, become mere <u>products of Socialism</u>, able to parrot the slogans but unable to think for themselves. The radical socialists have worked very hard to gain control of the great universities, the courts and the news media. They must control the news because if the people find out what is really happening, they might rebel, so if the socialists gain control of the news media, it becomes a mere propaganda machine. DECEPTION!

The middle class, those people who are innovators, self-starters, thinkers, must be decimated or eliminated because they will always oppose a government takeover.

SOCIALISM BUYS THE SOULS OF THE PEOPLE. They begin to look to the government more and more to supply all their needs. A person who does not work for a period of time and is supported wholly or partially by the government, loses his work ethic. It becomes very hard to go back to work. Even Christians begin to replace their trust and confidence in God with trust and confidence in big government. Whenever a problem shows up, they say, "The government should do something about that." Unconsciously, many times they put the government in the place of God or personal responsibility. SATAN USES THIS TO PREPARE THE PEOPLE FOR HIS ONE WORLD GOVERNMENT. DECEPTION.

The laws of free enterprise and lack of government intervention allow any individual or small business to grow and prosper. As they grow, they employ people. There is production in the country so the money of that country has value because it is backed by goods and services. Money is just paper unless it is backed by goods and services. However, Capitalism requires a righteousness in the society that only a spiritual awakening can provide.

Most governments today are a combination of capitalism and socialism. But the deception of false security allows the people to stray away from God. As socialism grows and capitalism diminishes. Socialism (through overtaxing and government controls) ruins opportunity so that it is very difficult for a poor man or a young man to get ahead. The politicians become entrenched and the way they protect their place is to decry the disparity between the rich and the poor, and as they redistribute the riches, they limit or ruin opportunities.

As Socialism encroaches more and more in the government, the big corporations and the very rich sidestep overtaxing because they have friends in government and lawyers and accountants that find the loopholes in the laws. The politicians begin to form a tight circle in which they all benefit from the "system". In lawmaking, they are encouraged or forced to vote with the party. The "party" keeps them in office. Any new politician who would like to establish justice is soon either bought off or run off. The <u>system</u> must be protected!

The people that support the socialistic system become like the chicken that follows her tormentor looking for corn or like the little kid who follows the bully because he is beating him up less now and even lets him eat part of his own lunch! The people actually vote for and even fight for the politicians who are keeping them poor! Satan "buys" the people's souls. They are being conditioned to accept THE NEW WORLD ORDER! DECEPTION!

CHAPTER SIX Ideologies and Our Defense

Satan is the great deceiver. He has been behind all the great deceptions we have seen in history. Each of those great deceptions were and are his <u>attempts to rule the world</u>. With every attempt the deception grows. Today we are engulfed in a time of deception in the entire world like nothing that has ever happened before. We can learn by the great and small deceptions that have engulfed whole societies in times past. We can also take very seriously the words of warning of our Lord and Savior Jesus Christ. *"Take heed that no man deceive you!"* The Scriptures from beginning to end show us the designs of Satan and his minions and also our own weakness to deception and how we need to stay close to God through Jesus our Lord. <u>Behind every design of deception in the history of mankind is Satan and his lies.</u> The book of Revelation shows how for a brief period of time, Satan, using the "beast" and the "false prophet" dominates the entire world for at least three and a half years, (some say seven).

The prophet Daniel spoke of this man who would deceive the whole world <u>for a season</u> in Daniel 11:36. "And the king shall do according to his will. And he shall exalt himself, and magnify himself above every god, and shall speak marvelous things against the God of gods, and shall prosper <u>till the indignation be accomplished. For that that is determined shall be done."</u> The New International Version says "– He will be successful until the time of wrath is completed" That's God's wrath, who will pour out his wrath upon this earth even using the hand of Satan to cleanse the earth. It will be a terrible time of evil brought about by the man of sin and the people who "received not the love of the truth" (II Thes. 2:10) At that time, the very last ones to be saved in the midst of terrible persecution and at the price of their very lives, will decide it's better to die than to follow Satan and be condemned and will surrender their lives to the Lord.

In Revelation 13:8 it shows how the deception will engulf the world: "And all that dwell upon the earth shall worship him whose names are not written in the book of life of the Lamb slain from the foundation of the world. If any have an ear, let him hear!" We must take heed and learn from the great deceptions, past and present in this world and the warnings that the Lord has given us in his Word. Daniel said: "The king shall prosper till the indignation be accomplished. For that which is determined shall be done!" God will allow this because of the ever increasing of mankind.

Today the master planners who work in the shadows (some are now in the open) want a One World Government or New World Order as they prefer to call it, believing that they will be the ones to control things. Nations and nationalism must be destroyed to create a One World Government. Justice and order must be destroyed in the nations. All free thinking must be destroyed because when people have the knowledge and freedom to think things through, they will choose freedom. (With the fervent desire of people to be entertained every minute of the day and the accessibility of electronics, people are forgetting how to think! They don't take time to think!) Families must be destroyed because through families, wisdom, values and order are passed on from one generation to another. An entire generation must be brought under this "mind control". Fear and indoctrination are used to control the people. The things we see playing out now through climate control, the green new deal, pandemic control, open borders, voter fraud, unlimited government spending, defunding the police, control of the courts, indoctrination in the schools and universities and the foreign policy fiasco are all part of a push to destroy the strength and freedom of every nation and more especially of the USA. If you study what is happening in different socialistic governments around the world, it looks like they are all reading from the same playbook! That's right! They are! The devil has worked from the beginning to rule the world.

Gender changing, promotion of homosexuality and brain washing the children instead of teaching the fundamentals in the schools are used to produce an ignorant generation that is bound up in its own vices and will accept this "freedom of values" in their "wonderful New World Order". This all is happening in the entire world but the concentrated effort is in the US because <u>this strong and free nation must be destroyed before they can subject the whole world to Socialism</u>, which will morph into the One World Government. Abortion, homosexuality, destruction of families and the pandemics are tools they use to reduce and control the world population.

Open borders, police defunding, wild government spending, the great "lock-down", changes in school curriculum and disastrous foreign policy are not the result of a fumbling president or adherence to some far-out ideas of the "squad". These are <u>well planned</u> and executed policies designed to prepare us for the "New World Order" where there is no sovereign nation, an ignorant populous, which will be limited in number to protect the planet and governed by a select few who are the "enlightened ones". We are being *seduced!*

God's purpose and desire is that evil should not take over. On the contrary, many times in the past God has raised up brave men and women that have stood strong and resisted and overcome evil. Hitler was defeated! Even at the apex of the power of the Soviet Union there were lights that could not be extinguished. Pastor Richard Wurmbrandt was imprisoned and tortured for 14 years, but they could not make him deny his faith in God. When he finally was liberated, he was still full of faith. He wrote the book "*Tortured for Christ*" and did much to wake up the world to the atrocities of Communism and help people who suffered from Communism through his organization VOICE OF THE MARTYRS.

All over the Soviet Union there were small groups here and there, underline studying the Word of God, one prisoner encouraging another with, "Jesus is the answer!" Christians had secret meetings and persecutors were sent to destroy them but the Christians testified to those sent to destroy their faith. Some persecutors were converted. In Poland, the people raise up a cross in a vacant corner lot. The Communist Regime tear it down; the people raise it up again. This happens again and again until the Regime lets them have their cross. In Russia, a Catholic priest continually encourages his people to trust in Christ. The Regime tortures and kills him, but they cannot kill the faith he inspired. Besides, though it wasn't manifest to the world, God was responding to the prayers of Christians inside and outside of that evil Communist Regime.

In Romania, a young pastor was preaching fiery sermons to inspire the people in their faith and to resist the regime. Many people were coming to his meetings. One night in the City Square of Timisoara, Romania, the people resisted the army. Many were cut down by the bullets and were crippled or killed, but the others kept singing Christian and patriotic songs and advancing, until the army ceased fire! The Communist dictator Nicolae Ceausescu fled in a helicopter. Not only that puppet government, but Romanian history was changed that night in the town square of Timisoara! These things happened all over the Soviet Union until one day the Berlin Wall came down and the Soviet Union crumbled! God did not allow that evil regime to continue at that time. There were those that "stood in the gap"!

In China while the "bamboo curtain" held that country completely isolated from the outside world from 1948 until 1983, Christians were imprisoned, pastors were tortured and killed, church buildings were confiscated or burned. They thought that they had "killed" the church! But when the curtain was opened in 1983 and outside Christians began to take Bibles into that suffering country, they found to their great surprise and joy, that the real church in China had multiplied a hundredfold! Christians were everywhere, in every walk of life! They were hungry for the Word of God!

What shall we say to these things? Shall the church go out with a whimper? Are we like the "flotsam" in the sea? Tossed about here and there until finally the Lord comes to rescue us? Or are we instruments of the living God, here with a purpose; lights in a darkening world, showing the way to those who are lost? The apostle Peter tells us that "God is not slack (concerning the return of Christ for his church) as some men count slackness, but is long suffering to us-ward, not willing that any should perish but that all should come to repentance". (2Peter. 3:9) It is time that the Church without spot or wrinkle should appear! Now is the time that many should be saved! We know not the day nor hour of his return, but we know that he commanded that we should "occupy till he returns!" Many have paid a great price in times past to preserve freedom and to overcome evil. Who knows if God will not grant us a reprieve in the midst of this Great Deception that has done such damage in the entire world now in our day?

We must understand the will and heart of God. He has given us a will and intelligence to decide and has given us his Word to guide and warn us. But if we insist in following Satanic doctrines and rebelling against our God and his Word, there comes a time that he says, "If you <u>insist</u>, I will let you go in your rebellion!" II Thessalonians 2:8: *And then shall that Wicked be revealed, whom the Lord shall consume with the spirit of his mouth, and shall destroy with the brightness of his coming: Even him who's coming is after the working of Satan with all power and signs and lying wonders, and with all deceivableness of unrighteousness <u>in them that perish; because they received not the love of the truth</u>, that they might be saved. And for this cause God shall send them strong delusion, <u>that they should believe a lie:</u> That they all might be damned who believed not the truth but had pleasure in unrighteousness.*

We need to love God and love the truth. Remember that temptations and deceptions are satanic in origin, even though it's people, movies, internet or any other media that tempt us. At the beginning Eve was tempted to believe that she was missing out on something that would make her greater and freer. Satan still uses the same tactics. The great delusions that we have examined from the Nazis and from the Marxists and now the Socialists have things in common. They all promise that you will get something that doesn't belong to you, like power and money. They promise a utopia without sweat and toil, and convince the people to take part in ushering in this great new world! There are also many who are not part of the "power group", but are very short sighted. They receive their little subsidies from the socialist government and that is all that interests them. They continually vote for socialism, even though socialism brings an ever-depressed economy. Government paternalism buys the soul of the people. It dulls their wits. They lose their identity and the power of an overcoming life.

CHAPTER SEVEN The Deception Grows

Satan wants to eliminate God from man's consciousness. The <u>Nazis</u> didn't seem to deny God but their god became Satan as they entered into deception. Then the <u>Marxists</u> tried to eliminate God. Now the <u>New World Order</u> is putting <u>man in the place of God</u>. It's worse all the time! We have allowed evolution to be taught in the schools for years without realizing the terrible damage it is doing to our children. Evolution has never been proved in 160 years and any thinking person can see that the marvels of creation would be impossible "by accident", and yet they teach it more and more as a "scientific" fact! Why? Because if we are an accident, then there is no God and if there is no God, all things are permissible! Who is to judge us? The deception is greater all the time. But Isaiah warns us, "Woe unto them that call evil good and good evil, that put darkness for light and light for darkness: that put bitter for sweet, and sweet for bitter! Woe unto them that are wise in their own eyes and prudent in their own sight!" (Isaiah 5:20)

We must understand that the One World Government that ushers in the reign of the "Beast" or the "Man of Sin" will be made up of <u>people</u> of flesh and blood and probably will be <u>voted in by the people democratically.</u> It's not going to appear out of the air! Deception has been growing and it has been and will be backed by a satanic power. We will concern ourselves however, mostly with the visible human part here on earth. Of course, even as in the deceptions of the past, men will be guided and controlled by satanic forces. Demons will have their part in blinding and controlling men and women to do their bidding. But we need to try to understand how it will play out here on earth. Those on the far left have worked diligently for many years to delete and destroy the truths and values that we have held dear. The terrible division of the people and the drastic changes in values of many people didn't happen overnight. For many years the far left has worked diligently to change these things <u>while the church slept.</u>

Think of the seemingly insurmountable task of getting the whole world to submit to one government and one man, even for a short while. They've been at it for some time now! To trace their progress, we list some of their accomplishments. This does not mean that everyone we mention here had a clear vision of bringing in the One World Government or even were aware of how their work was helping Satan work out his plans. Some did and some didn't, but Satan has been behind it all.

In 1918 President Woodrow Wilson's League of Nations was to maintain a permanent peace in the world, a peace controlled by man. John Dewey, many times called the "Father of modern education", taught that we shouldn't teach absolutes and should let the student learn what he wants to, that to curb certain tendencies would "warp" his personality. He started schools down the road of non-education, which has progressed into indoctrination of the socialistic mind set instead of education. The Communist Party was getting a foothold in the US. During the government of Franklin D Roosevelt, one Communist wrote to his collaborators in Europe, "We have an open door to the government here now!" Roosevelt's New Deal program didn't restart the economy as he was told it would, but it did make a good start on teaching the populous to depend on the government for their living. Madelyn Murray single handedly got prayer and Bible reading eliminated from schools. The "entitlement" system of social justice has been growing for years teaching the people that they are entitled to life-long government subsidies when in reality they need to go to work.

The liberal Supreme Court of the 70's <u>ignored the Constitution</u> and ruled in favor of abortion. The Supreme Court and the lower courts' overreach in many areas turned the court into a governing body instead of limiting themselves to judging laws to determine if they were according to the Constitution. For many years after the Roe vs. Wade decision, the courts began to in effect <u>change laws</u> by their decisions.

The feminist movement taught that women are the same as men. Of course, women have just as many rights as men. But God made women different, with different rolls to play in the family, in the society and before God. Women have a different body, from top to bottom, a different voice, a different perspective, a different emotional system. God made man and woman in his image. Man has half and woman has the other half. It is pure foolishness to say they are the same. Out of the evil roots that were established through the feminist movement has grown all manner of foolishness to the point of believing that a child is not born with a gender. It's up to the child to decide! The apostle Paul stated, "Professing themselves to be wise, they became as fools!" (Ro. 1:22)

The black community has been isolated from the rest of society and children separated from their fathers instead of being helped by the social services and entitlement programs. Women were encouraged to say they were single mothers so they could receive more child support. The black people were taught that they were victims, instead of encouraging industry and business to help get work for them. Single mothers began to multiply. The black family culture was being destroyed. Unwed mothers and crime among the black communities multiplied in direct proportion to the increase in the entitlement programs.

Those that think of themselves as controllers of world destiny, the elite, the *shadow government* say to themselves, "How can we <u>save the planet from over populating and subject all the peoples</u> in preparation for our One World Government? The world has many the different religions, nations and races, some are at total enmity one with another. The *controllers* believe that the sense of nationalism and faith in God <u>have to be broken</u> or surpassed with a <u>stronger emotion.</u>"

The charter of the United Nations was drafted in August of 1941 and signed into being in June of 1945 at the end of World War II. Its concept seemed good: to maintain world peace and welfare. But God resisted the tower of babel for a reason. It was man's salvation of man. They were going to reach heaven (reach that utopia) by uniting man without God. The UN seemed good to human reason, but without God, we will never achieve world peace and welfare. The UN soon became infested with rogue states and their ideas. Some of the countries with the very worst human rights records are on the security council and each one has veto rights. Each country has one vote, regardless of their bad record and regardless of how much they contribute to the expenses of the UN. So, in effect, the rogue states rule. The UN has a terrible record. They have never solved international conflicts. The UN and its subsidiaries have done more to promote the socialist and communist agenda than any good they might have done. By now it is apparently another vehicle made to order to help usher in the One World Government. UNESCO continually solicits donations to help the poor, but if people knew how much evil UNESCO has promoted, they wouldn't give them money. Much of that money ends up in the wrong hands.

The great universities have had a major role in changing the American mentality and the very direction of our nation. Parents, eager to give their children the best opportunity have stretched their budget and worked overtime. They have taught their children the necessity of a "higher" education. Meanwhile the big universities, while receiving huge subsidies and grants from the government and rich endowments, have been charging exorbitant tuition, often leaving the students themselves deeply in debt when they graduate, while the professors work very hard to destroy the young people's faith in God and indoctrinate them to be citizens of the "new" society! What they are <u>not</u> doing is making better people out of the students!

My brother was in a class of freshman students in the Greeley Colorado's teacher's college (1956) when the professor said, "Why do dogs not believe in eternal life?" (Stupid question, but no one could think of a good answer.) "Because they don't know they are going to die! Class dismissed!" Neither the question or the answer was based on reason. Dogs do not even have the same capacity of reason that man has, nor the ability to communicate what they think, but the green young students were baffled. That kind of insidious "teaching" was only the beginning of the barrage of indoctrination they would continue to receive, designed to destroy their faith, while they are receiving their "higher education "! Then after years of indoctrination, the students are released onto society, carrying a big back pack of unjust debt and an ideology their parents didn't have and they themselves do not deserve or even fully understand. But like the little boy that follows the bully, they parrot what their professors taught them, taking part in the great DECEPTION! We must add here that this scenario is not universal. There are many very good and common-sense professors that have constantly held against the current, and have taught their students how to think for themselves.

Many people who collaborate with this *Ideology* (man's salvation of man) do not even realize where this is all going, but have been convinced that the "other side is mistaken." It is evident that *the shadow government* is working on several specific things in preparation for this New World Order to come into its fullness: 1) Eliminate God from the consciousness of man; 2) Bring all the nations to their knees economically and militarily. 3) Destroy national and individual identity and citizenship. Being a world citizen is completely vague. What language do you speak? What are your values? Who are your people? What is your identity? Without a self-identity people have no initiative or purpose. It even leads many people to suicide. The people must be made to believe they need help from a world government because even national government is inadequate. 4) Reduce and control the world population; we must "save our planet". A tree or an animal become as important as a person or even more important (unless of course he or she is of the *elite class*). 5) Destroy the fabric of society. The family and faith in God must be destroyed.

FEAR and DIVISION are two of the tools they use to control of the people and bring all the peoples of the world under subjection; fear of a terrible disease, fear of war, fear that the planet will not sustain us, fear of economic depression. And divide and conquer. The news is always filled with fearful things. All nationalism must be destroyed and the people divided into all kinds of groups, ethnic, religious, color of skin, political parties, etc. Some current "movements" that are working together to achieve these goals are; Black Lives Matter, LGBT, Critical Race Theory. The values, and national history have to be destroyed in order to destroy confidence and loyalty to our nation and our culture. They destroy and divide in order to control.

The corporate media (so called Main Stream News) has been bought up by a few very rich people and has become one of the most powerful tools of the far left. All those things put together have the common goal to reduce an entire generation to fearful ignorance, soft and pliable in the hands of their "masters". A people without a will of their own. People whose implanted ideology has made them stupid, unable to discern between logic and chaos or between right and wrong. DECEPTION!

"Scientific" politicized misinformation has replaced true science. "Save the Planet" and fear of the Pandemic, though both things have some basis in fact are grossly exaggerated in order to control the people and to ruin the economies.

Christians should be good stewards of God's creation and also maintain good health practices but with a confidence that if we are careful and do our part, God will preserve us and has made this planet with sufficient resources to supply all that we need until he makes all things new.

They say the planet cannot support us, but consider this; much of the land is waste and could be productive. They say we will run out of water, yet three fourths of the planet is water. God could suck water out of the ocean and cause it to rain over the dry land and change the capacity of productivity of the globe in a short time! But the sin of mankind is why some go hungry and thirsty while others get too fat. Now more than ever before, we need to put our trust in God more than in the so-called science which in fact is <u>not even remotely scientific</u>.

CLIMATE CHANGE; first, "Science" warned us that within two generations the entire globe would freeze over. Then they realized that the climate in general was getting warmer. So "Science", doing a complete flip, warned us that withing 50 years the globe would heat up so much that the oceans would overflow and the "green-house" effect would destroy our way of life. That was fifty years ago.

Many computer models were set in the seventies by the United Nations (programmed by men). These programs have already been proven totally wrong, but they don't tell the public that. The warming trend stopped a number of years ago. True information does not help their "narrative". Much of what the public is told is partly or totally false. Several years ago, the Mississippi River froze over solid, the first time in many years. It seems to be getting cooler again! Now they have changed the name to "climate change", but they still teach that it's going to destroy us!

The climates of the world have suffered changes since the beginning of time, long before man was using fossil fuels. They say that the ice caps on both arctics are melting away. That may be true but a change in temperature from minus 50% to minus 48% is not going to melt much ice! If the ice caps are indeed melting, it's because it is heating up from below! Only God has control of that! It should remind us to repent rather than believe the falsely so-called science! When scientists begin to promote an ideology instead of studying true science, it is no longer true science.

But God said in Genesis 8:22 *"While the earth remaineth, seed time and harvest, and cold and heat, and summer and winter, and day and night shall not cease."* We can trust in God's promise! Our confidence is in God. He uses climate change to warn man of coming judgment, but he will take care of his own until the end!

COVID 19 PANDEMIC! It comes to light now that for years in China, they were experimenting with *gain of function* of several viruses. (Increasing the function or capacity of virus!) They were making these viruses more dangerous! Why? Money was coming in from all over the world for this project. It became obvious that they were <u>not</u> experimenting on how to <u>cure</u> the virus because when it broke out, no one had a clue of what to do to cure or mitigate the effects of it! Immediately when it broke out, the Communist Party closed off that province from all the other provinces in China while leaving free air travel to the rest of the world! The World Health Organization announced that the virus was <u>not dangerous</u>. Then as soon as the virus was spread to much of the world, WHO announced that the whole world should be shut down to avoid the spread of this deadly virus! Does that make sense? Are the planners and controllers really helping us?

Hospitals were shut down from attending other medical needs in order to attend this dangerous virus. People were advised that there was <u>nothing they could do</u> if they have the virus because antibiotics do not affect a virus. "Stay at home until you are about to die and then go to a hospital where they can put you on a ventilator and give you a 50% chance of recovering!" Also, "protocol" had sick people standing out in the weather six feet apart for hours waiting medical attention. (The sick would get very sick of course!) Other serious deceases were "put on hold". No one knows nor will know how many died from lack of attention to all the other deceases, or because of the "protocol". We have no statistics on these things we mention, but with common sense we can see that these were not good health practices and would cause more sickness and death instead of less.

Early, effective treatment that good doctors and many common-sense people were discovering were not being made known and in many cases this valuable information was being suppressed. Most of the deaths for a year from many different causes were attributed to Covid19, adding to the fear! Does that sound like the government agencies doing their best to protect the welfare of the people through good sound scientific information?

Meanwhile some honest doctors and scientists were experimenting and discovering that there are indeed a number of cheap remedies and medications available to mitigate the virus. In China those doctors disappeared! In the rest of the world, they were put to silence and "investigated". For much time the official rules and propaganda have denied and prohibited the use of these simple remedies. No one knows how many deaths have been <u>caused</u> in fact by the misinformation and rules set down in the name of "protecting the people" from this terrible pandemic! One thing is certain, however, that much power and control over the people was gained through all this! Plus, the world population was lowered. That's progress?

TWO OPPOSING VISIONS, THE ENGINES BEHIND THE "GREAT DIVIDE"!

<u>Containment or Non-containment (or) Bible view or Evolution view</u>

<u>The Biblical view</u> of mankind is that man is made in the image of God and therefore capable all kinds of good, including producing to supply all his needs and governing himself, but has a sin nature that must be limited and contained. Therefore, man will produce and prosper when he has freedom to act, but in order to <u>contain</u> the evil, there is a need for just laws and law enforcement on the one hand, and on the other, a need for open competition, a need to <u>limit government</u> and a need for a strong military in order to protect the nation from external evil forces which will certainly arise from time to time.

<u>The Evolution view</u> is that there is no God, man is an accident and came from nothing, but now has evolved into something better; a super intelligent animal, almost a god. Not only is this new being more intelligent, (he or she or it) is a better person. The problem of evil is brought on by laws and restrictions and unequal distribution of the "pie" of goods of this world. If the poor just had more money and better

living conditions, and if there were fewer of them, and if there was no sense of guilt, they would be very good. Of course, in this process of evolution, <u>there are the elite</u>, who have evolved much more than their fellows and now are in charge of the continued evolution. They will also be in charge of limiting the population so that this planet will not be overpopulated. The first to have to be eliminated are those that oppose this view. Man must be freed of the guilt complex and live a life "free of values" thus eliminating sin! Right and wrong will be judged on a daily basis of how it seems right for those involved in that moment. The elite will now guide the evolution process into the New World Order where everyone will be happy in this new value free society where <u>anything goes</u>! Of course, everyone following this ideology does not have a fully developed philosophy like we just described, but they are buying into it and following blindly those that lead them.

<u>But we know that only those that love and want to obey God will enter in to the kingdom of Heaven.</u> Satan came to deceive and destroy. His plan and desire from the beginning was to wrench control from God and control the world. He plans to take over by force and deception. <u>Fear, division, false premises</u> and <u>control of the people</u> have been instruments in each of the great deceptions we have studied. That is because the Great Deceiver, Satan, is behind each one of them. As the deception grows, God's message is "Beware that you not be deceived!" (Mathew 24: 4 paraphrased) and let us therefore cast off the works of darkness, and let us put on the amour of light!" (Romans 13:12)

HOW CAN WE KNOW THE TRUTH? Fear not! God has given us his

Word in the Bible to know the truth. Jesus said, "If you abide in my Word (diligently study and obey the Bible) you shall know the truth, and the truth shall set you free!" We need not fear if we are walking close to Jesus and obeying his Word!

CHAPTER EIGHT 666, Is it just a Number?

We need to understand that the New World Order is not just about one man ruling the entire world. That will come to pass, but it would be impossible without a drastic change in the mentality of the people. It has to be a <u>worldwide mentality</u>. It's all about salvation from all our many woes by man. We have been observing the deceptions of the past and the attempts to take over the world by evil men. Satan has been behind each of these great efforts.

Now many world leaders are talking about this New World Order, some of them claim to be Christians. Unfortunately, many are following these world leaders. We need to wake up and realize that the ambition of Satan from the very beginning was to seize control of God's creation. The second Psalm speaks very clearly of this rebellion. Verse three especially, *"Let us break their bands asunder and cast away their cords from us."* The Woke movement is the epitome of this rebellion against God and his Word and Christian values, even to the point of changing the God given sex. The first Christians in Jerusalem understood that the second Psalm was speaking about the rebellion of the Jewish nation against Christ. (Acts 4:25-28) Now we see that this Psalm applies to the whole world! The master planners want to throw off the limitations that God has given us for our own good.

Six is the biblical number for man. 666 is not only about one man. It is a system of beliefs that man is in charge of his own salvation. On this world stage will appear a winsome man, very charismatic, who will seem to have the solution to peace and safety. The people (who have been deceived) will say "He is the one that will save us!" And they will worship him and even worship Satan. (Revelation 13:4 and 8 paraphrased) 666 is the mark of the beast. Six is the spiritual number for man. 666 is man, man, man. The writer of Revelation instructs us to use our intellect to understand about that seal. It's not just about three digital numbers, <u>it's about the total control and salvation of man without God.</u> Now as the first Christians saw that the second Psalm spoke of the Jewish rebellion, we should see that it speaks of the world-wide rebellion against God and his Christ!

While the world is gripped in fear and conditioned to believe that government is their salvation, this tremendous charismatic man will appear and he will work together with the false prophet to promise peace and prosperity in all the earth and a new type of religion to <u>unite all the different religions of the world</u>. Miracles will be done through these men, but they will be *"signs and lying wonders"* (2 Thess. 2:9) The entire scenario will seem to be good and this man will certainly not appear like a beast. On the contrary, many people will even think he is the Christ. (The statue of a terrible looking beast in front of the UN building, if it has a purpose, it is to make the people think that the beast will look like that!) This handsome, winsome man will not look like that! He will *deceive* the people! The apostle John saw the beast *"rise up out of the sea"* The sea speaks of the multitudes of the earth. The Satanic system and the man will be accepted and talked about by everybody! The seven heads and ten horns speak of a political system, nations and kings. The sad thing is that it rises up out of the sea; it's widely accepted by everyone!

Everybody except those that truly believe in God and fear God will believe him. At the same time, they will be taught that there is no sin. That is why it is called "a value free life!" Changing the meaning of words and making phrases that make evil sound good is part and parcel of the strategy to beguile the people. 666 is <u>a system</u> that people are <u>learning to accept</u> without realizing that the reign of the beast is a <u>system of government</u> and not merely a digital number. The great deception doesn't happen in one minute, it has been gaining power and acceptance slowly for many years, but now more than ever it is happening before our eyes!

We must understand the mindset of the "Designers of the New World Order". They believe that the evolution of man has now reached a stage in which man himself is in charge of it. But the apostle Paul writes, *"When they say peace and safety, then sudden destruction will come upon them as travail upon a woman with child, and they shall not escape!"* (I Thessalonians 5:3)

In the schools they are replacing fundamental subjects with a curriculum that normalizes fornication, homosexual activities, choosing what sex they want to be and teaching them that they do not have to obey their parents. (But yes, they should believe and obey the almighty State!) The State is more and more taking over the raising of children. We now have; kindergarten, prekindergarten, kindergarten for the three-year-olds and baby care. The State wants to take over child raising. Child Care is a big thing on the proposed national budget. If a child has a problem, he must go to see a psychologist. Common sense and/or parental guidance and discipline are not considered.

Television and the electronic devises are used in the classes and teaching is more and more controlled from the centers. Parents ignorantly take part in the deception, thinking that children are now smarter than their parents and so they can no longer teach their children. Now the "experts" must teach their children! So, the "State" takes over the raising of children at an ever more tender age in order to indoctrinate an entire generation. DECEPTION!

Young criminals burn down cities and they say, "They are peacefully protesting!" Criminals are turned loose from prisons and innocent people are punished! They say, "We are now gods, we can decide what is right and what is wrong!" *"Professing themselves to be wise, they became as fools!"* (Romans 1:22) When it seems that there is no remedy for the chaos they have caused, this soft-spoken winsome man will seem to have a magic solution and bring "peace and safety!" The Almighty State will take the place of God! The Bible warns us that in 2Timothy 3:1 *"Know this also, that in the last days PERILOUS TIMES SHALL*

COME. *For men shall be lovers of their own selves, covetous, boasters, proud, blasphemers, disobedient to parents, unthankful, unholy, without natural affection, truce breakers, false accusers, incontinent, fierce despisers of those that are good, traitors, heady, high-minded, lovers of pleasures more than lovers of God; having a form of godliness, but denying the power thereof. From such turn away."*

Jesus said in Mathew 24:15 *"When ye therefore see the ABOMINATION OF DESOLATION, spoken of by Daniel the prophet, stand in the holy place, (whoso readeth let him understand) flee".* He was of course talking first of all to the Jews, and of the Man of Sin claiming to be God and entering into the Temple in Jerusalem, but we are seeing churches accepting, allowing and even preaching the abominations of LGBT, Critical Race Theory, Green New Deal and etc.

The church of Jesus Christ represents the Holy Place today in our land and the <u>abomination that makes desolate</u> is being allowed into the church. Jesus said *"Ye are the light of the world!"* (Mt. 5:14) <u>The world has no other light</u>. He also said, *"When the light that is in you is darkness, how great is that darkness!"* (Mathew 6:23) If the light of the world (the church) is darkness, how great is that darkness in the world!

JESUS SAID, "BLESSED IS HE THAT HUNGERS AND THIRSTS AFTER RIGHTEOUSNESS, FOR HE SHALL BE FILLED!" (Mathew5:6) It is so important that we desire with all our hearts to know the truth. Not that we will always know all the truth of every situation or philosophy, but God knows our hearts if we desire to know the truth. He will protect us from deception and in good time reveal to us the truth that we need to know. Humility is so important in this. People fall into false teachings and false concepts because of <u>spiritual pride</u> or because <u>they want to be with the crowd</u> and so accept what everyone is saying without examining to see if it be true or false. Even when they should realize that it is an error, they won't admit it <u>because they do not want to be proven wrong</u>.

On the other hand, there are those who falsely proclaim to have the mind of God and lead the people astray. They say, "We understand these new doctrines and concepts because we are more advanced than the others!" They are full of spiritual pride and they themselves are victims of deceit! FALSE TEACHERS AND PROPHETS

We should be very humble before God! Note that the reason that God sends strong delusion is because "_they received not the love of the truth!_" and they "_took pleasure in unrighteousness_". (2 Thess. 2:10, 12) We repeat that one of the definitions of ideology is "a system that derives ideas exclusively from <u>sensation</u>." _It just feels right! And with the crowd, we have such a sense of power!_" Deception!

Jesus in his dissertation about the end of the ages, said, "_And because iniquity shall abound, the love of many shall wax cold, but he that shall <u>endure unto the end, the same shall be saved</u>!_" (Mathew 24:12-13) and "_Take heed to yourselves, lest at any time your hearts be overcharged with surfeiting_ (to indulge in anything to an excess) _and drunkenness, and cares of this life, and so that day come upon you unawares. For as a snare shall it come on all them that dwell on the face of the whole earth. <u>Watch therefore and pray always, that you may be accounted worthy to escape all these things that shall come to pass and to stand before the Son of Man</u>._" (Luke 21:34-36)

We are now living in a time of deception like none other. There have been great deceptions in time past, several of which we described in this book, but never has it been so general in all the world! Never have the mainstream news services worked together to hide the truth and present a false understanding of current events as they are doing today. It seems that now just a few people can control to a large extent the what most of the people know and how they think.

The governments of the world have taken control of many aspects of life, using fear of the Pandemic and Climate Change to subjugate the people. The disastrous results of the lock down are yet to be known, using <u>so-called science and fear</u> to subjugate entire nations. Truth is distorted or completely changed. But the truth is out there. We need to be diligent to seek the truth. There are honest doctors and scientists who are urgently trying to get out the truth about the pandemic, the vaccines, natural immunity and good remedies at reasonable prices. For example, baking soda is very cheap and kills virus in the mouth, where it first multiplies! Ivermectin, a long-proven drug for malaria has been successful as a prophylactic or very early after infection. Unfortunately, the very institutions that are supposed to be guiding and protecting the people are covering up much of the truth. The people are being trained to obey what is largely a false narrative so that the fear of disease, the fear of war and the fear that the world will be overpopulated and we will all starve, <u>dominate the will of the people.</u>

The shadow government of the world, those that pull the strings, have a plan: eliminate God, keep the people in ignorance and fear, institute the New World Order. The culmination of Satan's plans and efforts are found in Revelation chapter 13 where the Antichrist takes control for three and a half years. In 13:5b it says concerning the Antichrist, "*...and power was given unto him to continue for forty and two months.*" *God gives him that time to deceive the people <u>who do not receive the love of the truth</u> and to consume God's wrath upon his enemies.* (2 Thessalonians 2:10)

The prophet Isaiah proclaimed "*Woe unto them that call evil good and good evil, that put darkness for light and light for darkness, that put bitter for sweet and sweet for bitter!*" (Isaiah 5:20) That is exactly what we are witnessing and The Devil's Great Deception is taking place today in America and in the whole world! So, we conclude by saying that 666 is first and foremost man, man, man. The danger of 666 is trusting in man's salvation from the problems that face us and not in God. Sometimes we just need to have patience while we sweat and toil to overcome our situation. People are being mentally prepared for big government salvation. Those that physically take the mark 666 would have already put their trust in man for some time, and they will be lost!

CHAPTER NINE Light in the Midst of Darkness

Where do we stand in our day? Are we to stand by and let the world wind down and then go out with a whimper? No! THE CHURCH OF JESUS CHRIST IS CALLED TO BE LIGHT in the midst of darkness and to be salt where there is no salt! Are we not called to bring grace where there is no grace? Are we not called to stand for the truth when all the world is believing a lie? The apostle Paul said, (2 Thessalonians 2:7) *"He that is restraining will restrain until he gets to be taken out of the way."* That is the Glorious Church filled with the Spirit of God. If you are just waiting to be "taken up", you may still be waiting when the Glorious Church is taken up! <u>Until we are taken up, we should restrain that evil and bring light</u>, so that all who can be saved will be saved! The Lord taught us to pray "Thy kingdom come on earth as it is in heaven." That means we should pray and work for the Kingdom to come here while we are yet here on earth! "Who knows if God may turn and bless us with a tremendous outpouring of his Holy Spirit and revival in these last days?"

"But ye brethren are not in darkness, that that day should overtake you as a thief. We are all children of light, and children of the day: we are not of the night, nor of darkness." (I Thess 5:3-5) And another council from Romans 12:2 *"And be not conformed to this world, but be ye transformed by the renewing of your mind that ye may prove what is the good and acceptable and perfect will of God."* And Isaiah 60: 1-2 says: ***"Arise and shine for thy light is come, and the glory of the Lord is risen upon you! For behold the darkness shall cover the earth and gross darkness the people, but the Lord shall arise upon you and his glory <u>shall be seen upon you!</u>"***

This world is under delusion, under deception. Now as never before Christians need to be grounded in the Word of God and the love of the truth! Jesus is coming back for his church that is <u>prepared</u>. Jesus said (Luke 21:36) *"Watch therefore and pray always, that you may be counted worthy to escape all these things that shall come to pass, and to stand before the Son of Man!"*

Where does the Glorious Church appear? I believe now as never before is the time that the Glorious Church without spot or wrinkle (Ephesians 5:27) and the Church of Philadelphia (Revelation 3:7-13) which is the same, shall appear in victory! Jesus said to the church in Philadelphia, the church of brotherly love, *"Because you have kept the Word of my patience, I will also keep thee from the hour of temptation which will come upon all the world, to try them that dwell upon the earth."* He promised to take the Philadelphia Church out of "the hour of temptation", and he said why; 1) they were the church of brotherly love, 2) they were keeping his Word, and 3) they did not deny his Name (they were Christians and let the whole world know it!) Now more than ever, God is preparing that bride for his coming. The Church of Philadelphia is the only church of the seven churches in Revelation with the promise as a body to be saved from the "hour of temptation" which will be the time described in Revelation when the wrath of God shall be poured out on this world system. (But there is a promise to the overcomers in each church.) (For more on this read my book, "The Bride, The Glorious Church", by Robert F Paden, Outskirts Press, or books2read.)

Our confidence is in God and his Word. *"What shall we then say to these things? If God be for us, who can be against us? He that spared not his own son, but delivered him up for us all, how shall he not with him also freely give us all things? Who shall lay anything to the charge of God's elect? It is God that justifieth. Who is he that condemneth? It is Christ that died, yea rather that is risen again, who is even at the right hand of God, who also maketh intercession for us. Who shall separate us from the love of Christ? Shall tribulation or distress, or persecution or famine, or nakedness, or peril, or sword? As it is written, 'For thy sake we are killed all the day long. We are counted as sheep for the slaughter'.*

Nay in all these things we are <u>more than conquerors</u> through him that loved us. For I am persuaded, that neither death, nor life, nor angels nor *principalities nor powers, nor things present, nor things to come, nor height, nor depth, nor any other creature, shall be able to separate us from the love of God, which is in Christ Jesus our Lord." (Romans 8:31-39)*

As the world goes from bad to worse, our hope is firm. Our anchor holds, because it holds on to the Solid Rock! There are two schools of thought at this time among committed Christians. One is that the world is no longer redeemable and all we can do is wait for the rapture. The other is that there will be a great awakening now and many in the world will turn to Christ.

There are so many in this world today that do not know their right hand from their left (spiritually speaking) Let us pray that God will have mercy and save many! Even to do as he commanded and to hear him say, "Well done, good and faithful servant! You have been faithful in few things; I will make you ruler over many things. Enter in to the joy of your Lord!" When the German girl, Sofia Scholl wrote "What does my death matter if by it thousands are awakened to stand up for the truth?" She was saying in effect, "There are things worth dying for!" What was Paul saying in effect? "We belong to Jesus and he will fulfill his eternal purpose for each of us if we remain faithful, so if we live or if we die, the Lord is with us!"

MARANATHA!

THE PLOWMAN

Also by Robert F Paden

The Life and Times of Robert F Paden
The Kid From Kansas in the Marine Corps

Standalone
Deception in Perilous Times
The Glorious Church The Bride

Also by The Plowman

The Kid From Kansas
Deception in Perilous Times
The Glorious Church The Bride

About the Author

About the auth

ABOUT THE AUTHOR

Robert F Paden (The Plowman) and his wife Bettye have been in missionary service for nearly half a century. First as Short-Term Assistants in Colombia, then in church planting in Argentina. They founded and ran a Children's Home for fourteen years in which nearly 400 children were cared for and helped for long or short periods of time. Currently, Robert is working with the Wichi aborigenes in northern Argentina.

The Paden´s celebrated their 65th wedding anniversary this year! They have four natural children and four adopted children, fifteen grandchildren and two great grandchildren!

Other books published by Robert are; THE KID FROM KANSAS and DECEPTION in Perilous Times.